Look Puzzle

The Great History Search

Kamini Khanduri

Illustrated by David Hancock

Designed by Ian Cleaver

History consultant: Dr Anne Millard

Series editor: Felicity Brooks

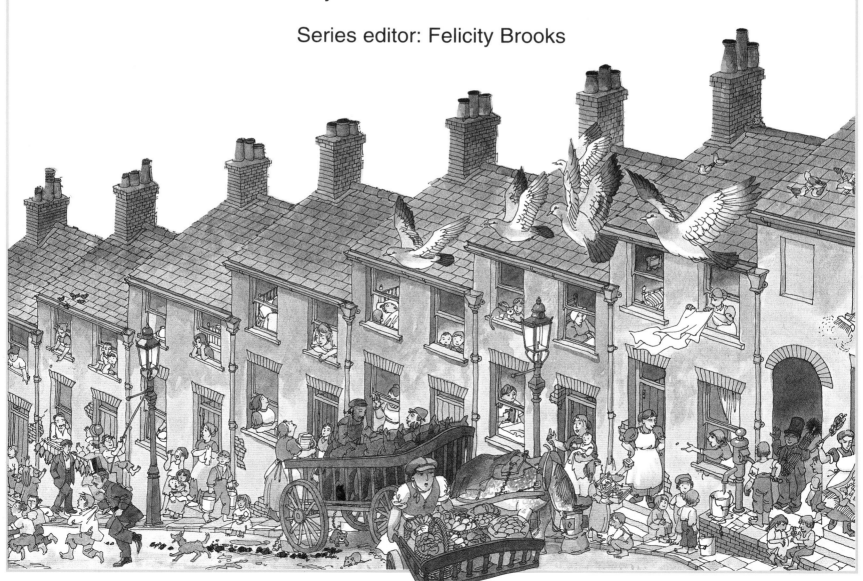

In the town on pages 34 and 35, some poor people lived in a workhouse.

On the American prairies on pages 36 and 37, many people rode in wagons.

Electric stoves were on sale in the department store on pages 38 and 39.

Turn to pages 32 and 33 to see all the people at the French ball in their best clothes.

You'll find this painting of a Dutch family on pages 30 and 31.

The Indian emperor on pages 28 and 29 sat on this beautiful throne.

The palace gardens were lit by paper lanterns at the Chinese party on pages 26 and 27.

Contents

The Incas on pages 24 and 25 played all kinds of musical instruments.

Jesters lived in medieval castles. See who else lived there on pages 22 and 23.

There was a dancing bear at the village fair on pages 20 and 21.

2

About this book

Early people painted pictures on their cave walls. See how they lived on pages 4 and 5.

In this book, you can find out about lots of different people and places from history. But this isn't just a history book, it's a puzzle book, too. This shows you how the puzzles work and gives a few tips to help you solve them.

The farmers on pages 6 and 7 used tools like this sickle.

This strip tells you the date. BC is before Christ and AD is after Christ.

Around the outside of each big picture, there are lots of little pictures.

The writing next to each little picture tells you how many of that thing you can find in the big picture.

This wagon in the distance counts.

People wrote on clay tablets in the Mesopotamian city on pages 8 and 9.

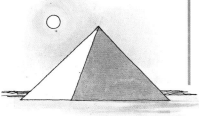

Find out how the Egyptians built pyramids on pages 10 and 11.

Part of this wall has been taken away, so you can see inside.

This part of a gun counts as one gun.

This cowboy coming out of the big picture counts as a little picture too.

Instead of spotting this printing press, you have to find where it is used.

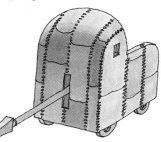

The Assyrians used siege engines in the battle on pages 12 and 13.

The puzzle is to find the people, objects and animals in each big picture. Some are easy to spot, but some are tiny, or hidden behind other things. If the big picture is in two halves (pages 4-5 and 12-13), you have to look in both halves. You'll find all the answers on pages 40-45.

Find out what the Vikings hung on their walls on pages 18 and 19.

Turn to pages 16 and 17 to find out why Romans took a flask of oil to the bath house.

People at the Greek market on pages 14 and 15 paid with coins like this one.

The old people told the children exciting stories. Can you find two storytellers?

Fish caught from the river were hung to dry on wooden frames. Spot 20.

Axes were stones on wooden handles. Find two.

People used these digging sticks to dig for roots in the ground. Spot three.

Baskets were woven from rushes. Find nine.

People made tools from stones called flints. Spot four other people chipping away at flints.

Early people

People shot animals with bows and arrows. Spot a boy who has shot a bird.

Early people moved around with the seasons, hunting animals and gathering plants to eat. The left-hand page shows some early people in Europe, spending the winter in a cave. The right-hand page shows them in summer.

People painted animal pictures on the cave walls. Spot three deer pictures.

Lamps were made by burning fur soaked in animal fat. Find five.

Women gathered berries in leather bags. Find three bags.

4

Men went hunting for wild animals. Find seven wild deer.

Skins and furs were sewn into coverings and clothes. Find five people sewing.

Babies were wrapped up warmly. Spot nine.

People scraped skins to clean them. Spot four skins being scraped.

Paint was made from soft rocks and animal fat. Find three people making paint.

People hung skins to dry on wooden racks. Spot five.

Antler

Some tools were made from antlers. Can you find four people carving antlers?

Necklaces were made from shells, stones, bones or teeth. Find 12.

People wore furs in winter and skins in summer. Spot a child being dressed.

Wooden spears with sharp flint tips were used for hunting. Spot 11.

Meat was roasted over a fire. Spot six people cooking.

First farmers

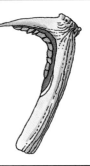

At harvest time, crops were cut down with tools called sickles. Spot five sickles.

Flat loaves of bread were baked on clay ovens. Can you spot eight ovens?

Wooden ladders were used for building. Find three.

Women fetched water from the stream. Find seven women with water pots on their heads.

Farming began when people learned to plant seeds and grow crops. They also tamed animals. These changes meant people could stay in one place instead of moving around. This is a farming village in the Middle East.

Spot three cooking pots.

Fish were caught in the stream. Spot four people fishing with nets.

People rolled out pieces of clay to make pots. Find two people making pots.

Men went hunting for wild animals. Spot two men coming back from a hunting trip.

Women made thread by spinning wool around a spindle. Spot three spindles.

The chief offered gifts to a statue of the village goddess. Find the statue.

Thatched roofs on houses caught fire easily. Find a roof on fire.

The grain from the crop was put into big baskets. Spot seven baskets.

Find two men mending the mud-brick wall around the village.

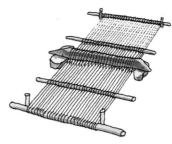

Thread was woven into cloth on a wooden frame called a loom. Spot three.

Sheep were kept for wool, milk and meat. Find 20.

Goats were kept for milk, skins and meat. Find four.

Pigs were kept for meat. Find six pigs and six piglets.

Cattle were kept for milk, skins and meat. Find 16.

Geese were kept for feathers, eggs and meat. Can you spot 11?

Children helped look after herds of animals. Find four herders with sticks.

Stones were used to grind grain into flour. Spot four women grinding.

Dogs helped with hunting and herding other animals. Spot eight.

Children scared birds away from the crops. Find four children scaring birds.

7

Living in cities

Most people couldn't read or write, so they hired scribes.
Spot one scribe.

Wheels were made from three pieces of wood joined together.
Can you spot ten?

Soldiers wore long cloaks and helmets, and carried spears.
Find 16.

Baskets were used for fruit, vegetables and grain.
Spot 14.

People used metal tubes as drinking straws. Spot four people using straws.

Furniture was made of wood.
Spot five chairs.

Early cities had temples, schools and lots of houses. This city is in Mesopotamia. The temple is on a big stepped platform, called a ziggurat. People are going there in a procession, to offer gifts to the city's god.

Buildings had flat roofs. Spot 40 people on rooftops.

Merchants used donkeys to carry packs.
Spot four with packs.

Rich boys went to school. Schools were very strict.
Spot a schoolboy sneaking in late.

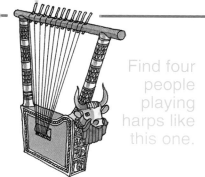

Find four people playing harps like this one.

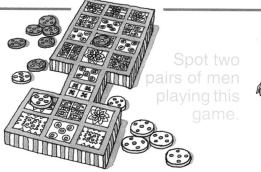

Spot two pairs of men playing this game.

Dresses were fastened at the shoulder. Find nine women in blue dresses.

People wrote on clay tablets. Spot someone running with a message on a tablet.

Find three metal-smiths who are pouring hot metal into hollow clay shapes.

The king ruled the city. Can you see him in his chariot with the queen?

Potters made clay pots on a wheel. Spot four potter's wheels.

Jars were used to carry wine. Find someone who has broken a jar.

People used seals to sign things. The picture on the seal was rolled onto soft clay. Spot one seal.

Stone seal

Rolling the seal

Picture on clay

Can you see a farmer bringing some sheep as a payment to the king?

Pyramids

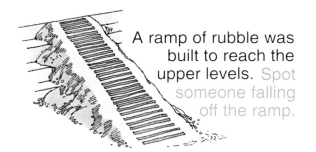

A ramp of rubble was built to reach the upper levels. Spot someone falling off the ramp.

The king and some other rich people kept pets. Find five dogs.

Grit

Spot four people polishing the blocks with stone tools and grit.

Polishing tool

The architect planned the building. Can you see him looking at his plans?

This is the doctor's tool basket. Find the doctor.

The queen had a pet monkey. Spot the monkey being naughty.

Ancient Egyptian kings and queens were buried inside big stone pyramids, which were built while they were still alive. There were no machines, so a pyramid took about 20 years to build. This one is in its early stages.

This is what the finished pyramid looked like. Find two models of finished pyramids.

Stonemasons used chisels to chip off rough edges. Can you find six?

Mallet

Chisel

The king came to check on the work. Can you see him being carried in his chair?

Find eight men using wooden poles to lever stone blocks into place.

Teams of men pulled the blocks along on sleds. Find nine sleds.

Carpenters used hammers to mend broken sleds. Spot six hammers.

Measuring instruments were used to check each block was level. Find five.

The queen would have her own pyramid beside the king's. Spot the queen.

Oil was used to help the sleds move smoothly. Spot four jars of oil.

The overseer was in charge of the building work. Can you see him pointing angrily with his stick?

Baskets were used for carrying rubble. Find a man with a hole in his basket.

Birds called hawks looked for food around the building site. Find seven.

Metalsmiths made and mended tools. Spot three saws like this one.

Scribes made lists of how many blocks and tools were being used. Spot six scribes.

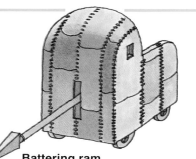
Battering ram

Siege engines with battering rams inside were used to break through the city walls. Spot five siege engines.

Can you find four horses swimming across the river?

Archers attacked with bows and arrows. Spot 12 bows.

Soldiers wore tunics, leggings and boots. Spot four soldiers putting on their boots.

Spot five soldiers carrying sacks full of stolen goods.

Going into battle

Some soldiers attacked with swords. Find 15 swords.

The Assyrian people had a big army of soldiers. The top part of this picture shows the soldiers marching into battle.

The bottom part shows them attacking a city. They stole things and captured people from the places they attacked.

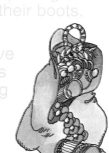

Many people were captured by the soldiers. Spot seven captives with their hands tied.

Some horses wore bright saddle cloths. Spot four yellow cloths.

There was fighting on top of the walls. Spot seven people falling.

12

The soldiers stole animals. Spot seven sheep being led away.

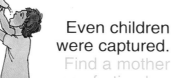

Even children were captured. Find a mother comforting her child with a drink.

The soldiers carried shields. Spot someone who has dropped his shield.

Inflated skins were used as floats to cross rivers. Spot someone who has let go of his float.

The king rode into battle in his chariot. Can you see him?

Soldiers used ladders made of wood. Can you find eight?

Many soldiers attacked with spears. Spot a broken spear.

Slingers attacked by hurling big stones from leather slings. Can you spot seven others?

Small boats were used to carry things across rivers. Spot four boats.

Scribes made lists of how many people had been killed or captured. Find two scribes.

Soldiers on horseback were called the cavalry. Spot two soldiers on white horses.

13

At the market

This coin is from Athens. Other cities had their own coins. Spot a man dropping all his money.

Officials checked the weight of things. Find six sets of weighing scales.

People ate olives and used their oil for cooking and in lamps. Spot someone eating olives.

Can you find four dogs?

Rich people shopped with their slaves. Spot a slave with too much shopping.

This picture shows a busy marketplace in the city of Athens in Greece. A Greek marketplace was called an agora. All the shops were under a covered area called a stoa. Out in the open, there were lots of stalls.

Soldiers had spears and big bronze helmets. Can you see five soldiers?

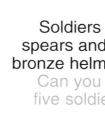

Cats were rare pets for rich people. Find four which have escaped.

Fish was a very popular food. Spot four people who have been to the fish stall.

 Find three children playing with hoops.

 The wine-seller let some people taste his wine. Spot four people drinking wine.

 Can you find three people carrying the sandals they have bought?

 Wise men called philosophers met to discuss science and politics. Spot two arguing.

 There were often statues of gods or famous people. Find two statues.

Lamps were the only lighting used in houses. Find the lamp stall.

People from outside the city had to change their money at the banker's stall. Spot the banker.

 Rich people bought slaves. Spot a slave who is trying to escape from his new master.

 Some people wore hats when it was sunny. Find five hats.

 Pottery was often beautifully painted. Spot five two-handled jars like this.

 Actors in plays wore masks like this. Find three actors going to a rehearsal.

15

The bath house

People used sticks called strigils to scrape oil and dirt off their bodies. Spot five.

To relax, people had their bodies massaged by a slave. Spot four people having a massage.

Lots of exercises went on at the baths. Find five people lifting weights.

Spot someone stealing another man's clothes from a changing room locker.

The hot room was called the caldarium. Can you find it?

The Romans made lots of statues. Can you find a statue of the emperor?

Roman towns had public bath houses, with hot, warm and cold baths. People went to bathe, but also to talk about business, to exercise, or just to gossip. A visit might last hours, and lots of people went every day.

Fighting men called gladiators were very popular. Spot this gladiator with all his fans.

Women went to a separate bath house. Find five women with their towels.

People wore sandals in the hot room, so as not to burn their feet. Spot a man who has forgotten his sandals.

Apartments near the baths were noisy. Find a man complaining about all the noise.

Instead of soap, people used oil to clean their bodies. Spot 11 oil flasks.

Find eight soldiers with their helmets.

Some floors were were covered with mosaics (pictures made from pieces of stone). Spot a mosaic floor.

Attendants worked at the baths. Find an attendant with a pile of towels.

Food, such as pastries and olives, was on sale. Spot two trays of food.

The cold room was called the frigidarium. Can you see where it is?

Can you see someone putting on a toga – a very big piece of material?

People paid to enter the baths. Spot a thief who has run off with someone's purse.

Most large bath houses had a library, with scrolls to read. Find the library.

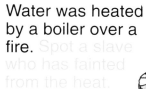
Scroll

Water was heated by a boiler over a fire. Spot a slave who has fainted from the heat.

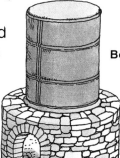
Boiler

17

Women fastened their tunics with brooches. Find someone doing up her brooch.

Firewood was kept outside. Spot two people gathering wood.

There were spoons and knives, but no forks. Find 12 spoons.

Women wore dresses with tunics on top. Spot someone with a torn tunic.

A poet called a skald played the harp and recited poems. Find the poet.

Winter feasts

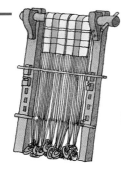

Cloth was woven on a big loom. Can you see the loom?

The Vikings lived in northern Europe. The men were fierce warriors who sailed abroad in their big ships.

At home, most Vikings lived in long houses, in small villages. Here, a village chief is giving a feast at his house.

The chief had his own chair. Can you find him?

Wool tapestries hung on the walls. Find a child hiding behind one.

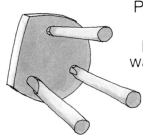

People sat on stools or on wooden platforms along the walls. Spot someone falling off a stool.

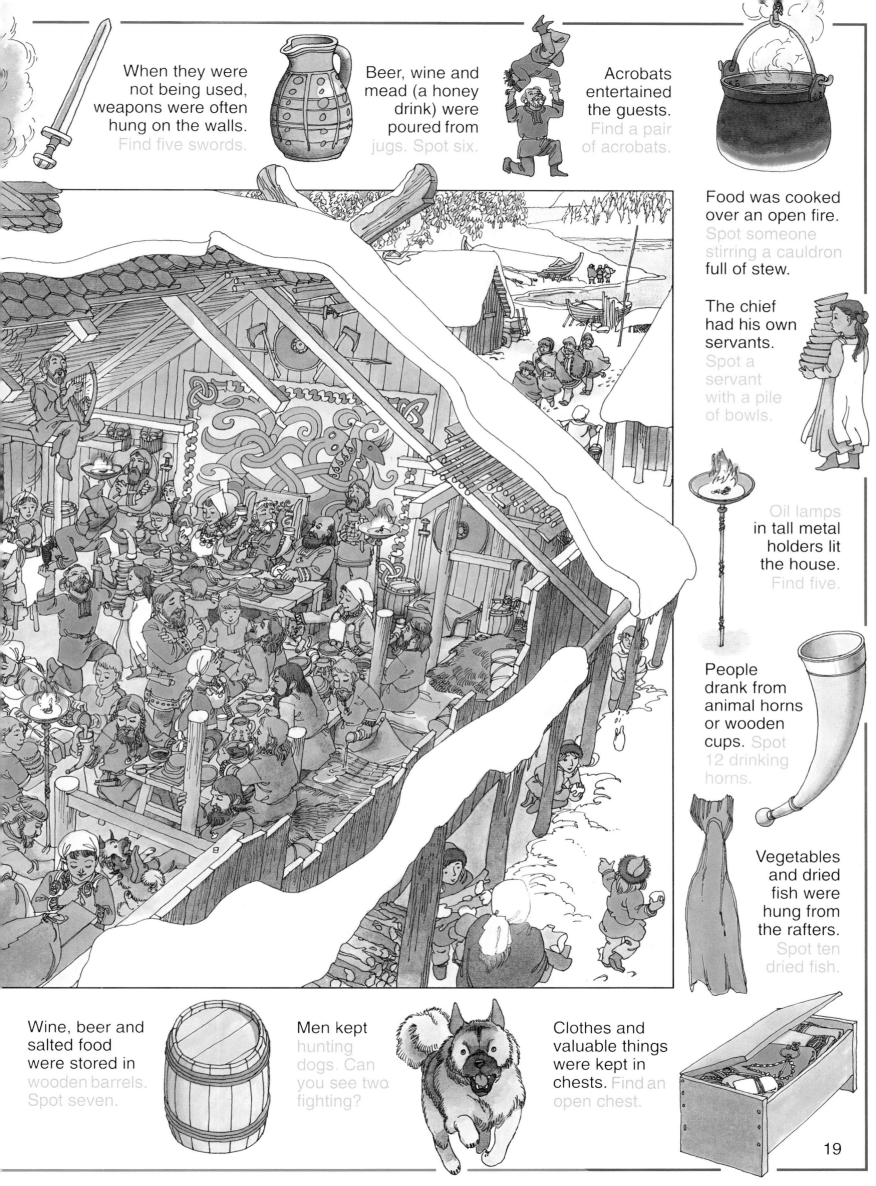

When they were not being used, weapons were often hung on the walls. Find five swords.

Beer, wine and mead (a honey drink) were poured from jugs. Spot six.

Acrobats entertained the guests. Find a pair of acrobats.

Food was cooked over an open fire. Spot someone stirring a cauldron full of stew.

The chief had his own servants. Spot a servant with a pile of bowls.

Oil lamps in tall metal holders lit the house. Find five.

People drank from animal horns or wooden cups. Spot 12 drinking horns.

Vegetables and dried fish were hung from the rafters. Spot ten dried fish.

Wine, beer and salted food were stored in wooden barrels. Spot seven.

Men kept hunting dogs. Can you see two fighting?

Clothes and valuable things were kept in chests. Find an open chest.

19

Village life

Can you see someone using stepping stones to cross the stream?

Merchants came to the fair from nearby towns. Spot a merchant unloading wine from a cart.

Hoe

Rake

Spade

Houses had vegetable plots. Spot someone using each of these tools.

Things for sale at the fair were put on tables. Spot four.

There were all kinds of entertainment at the fair. Find a dancing bear.

Stocks

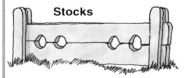

People who did wrong were punished. Spot a man with his legs in the stocks.

In the Middle Ages, most of the people in Europe lived in small villages. A few villagers owned their own land. The rest lived and worked on land owned by a lord. In this English village, the summer fair is being set up.

The lord lived in a big house or a castle. Can you see him setting off on a hunting trip?

People went to church often. Spot the priest sweeping the church porch.

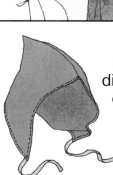

People wore different kinds of hats. Spot ten pointed hoods.

The blacksmith made and mended metal tools. Can you find him?

Can you see three people chopping wood outside their houses?

Milk was made into butter in a churn. Spot two churns.

Everyone had their grain ground into flour at the village windmill. Can you see it?

People kept bees for honey. Spot a man being chased by a swarm of bees.

Chickens were kept for meat, feathers and eggs. Spot two people feeding chickens.

Find the miller taking money for grinding some grain.

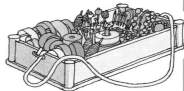

Can you spot someone going around selling small things from a tray?

Lots of things were bought and sold at the fair. Spot a big pile of cheeses.

Cats were useful for catching rats and mice. Find nine other cats.

Most people had fleas and head lice. Find a woman picking lice from her child's hair.

Castle life

In the Middle Ages, kings and lords in Europe built castles. The strong, stone walls kept enemies out, but castles were often cold, damp places to live in. These pages show part of a castle and the people living there.

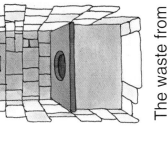

The waste from toilets dropped down to the ground below. Can you find two toilets?

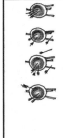

Prisoners were kept in the dungeon. Spot a prisoner in chains.

Servants were always busy. Spot a servant with a tray of goblets.

There was enough food stored to last months. Spot the storeroom.

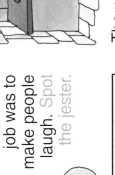

The jester's job was to make people laugh. Spot the jester.

Spot 20 guards on the battlements, looking out for enemies.

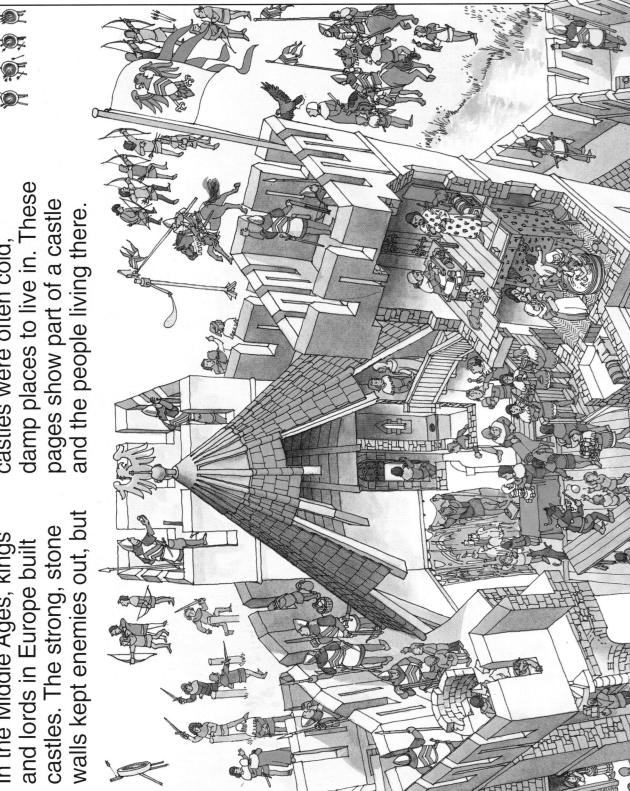

The lord and his wife slept in a big bed with curtains all around it. Find the bed.

This is the lord. Can you see him in his office, counting out his money?

Fierce birds called falcons were trained to hunt. Find three.

People didn't wash often. Spot someone in a bathtub.

22

Knights on horseback trained to fight with long spears called lances. Find four.

Tapestries helped keep out the cold. Spot someone hanging a tapestry.

Musicians called minstrels played from a gallery. Can you see them?

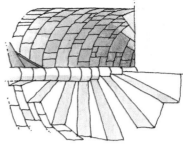

The castle had stone spiral staircases. Spot someone falling down the stairs.

Windows had shutters on the inside. Spot someone looking out of a window.

Find ten archers at shooting practice with their bows and arrows.

Water was pulled up in buckets from a well. Spot the well.

Find three horses looking out of their stables.

Guards who were off duty rested in the guardroom. Find the guardroom.

Everyone had a job to do. Can you see the candle-maker?

The priest held religious services in the chapel. Can you find it?

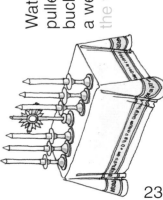

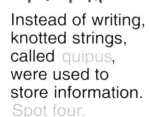

Buildings were made from stone blocks which fitted together perfectly. Spot four storehouses.

The soft wool from alpacas was used to make clothes. Find eight.

Bridges were made out of reeds. Spot two.

Women often carried babies on their backs. Find eight babies.

Instead of writing, knotted strings, called quipus, were used to store information. Spot four.

Inca homes

Guinea pigs were not pets, but were kept for meat. Can you find 12?

The Incas lived in the Andes mountains of South America. They built cities and strong stone roads. In this farming village, people are growing crops of corn and potatoes on terraces (steps of land dug into the mountainside).

Llamas were used to carry packs. Find a llama sitting down.

Messengers called chasquis ran quickly to deliver messages. Spot four.

Trumpets called pototos were made from shells. The sound carried far. Find one.

Looms had a strap, which went around the weaver's back. Spot three.

Sandal soles were made of llama skin. Find someone putting on some sandals.

This big mountain bird is a condor. Spot another one.

Spot someone making a drink called chicha by spitting chewed fruit into water.

Potatoes grew well on the high slopes. Find ten sacks of potatoes.

Wooden sticks like this were used for digging. Find ten digging sticks.

Women made flour by grinding corn between stones. Spot a woman grinding.

Cooking pots were all shapes and sizes. Find one like this.

Children scared birds away from the crops by firing stones from slings. Find two slings.

Musical instruments were played on special occasions. Spot each of these.

Panpipes

Drum

Flute

The Inca emperor was a strict ruler. Can you see him in his litter, coming to inspect the village?

Litter

A Chinese party

People used fans to keep cool. Spot three fans.

Chinese emperors and noblemen lived in beautiful palaces with lovely gardens. Most other people in China were poor. In this picture, a rich nobleman is having a firework party. He is sitting on the veranda with his wife.

Pottery, clothes and furniture were often decorated with dragon pictures. Find eight.

Silk covers were draped over chairs. Find four chair covers.

People ate rice with almost every meal. Find a half-finished bowl of rice.

Incense burner

People burned incense to make a sweet smell. Spot an incense burner.

Many people kept pet dogs. Find seven.

Wood was often covered with a shiny substance called lacquer. Find seven lacquered trays.

Find the palace gardener and his children watching the fireworks.

Gong

Drum

Flute

Musicians entertained the guests. Spot these musical instruments.

Men and women wore silk robes. Find eight red robes.

Fireworks were invented in China. Spot a servant lighting a firework.

Paintings on silk or paper scrolls were hung on walls. Find two.

Officials took notes at important events. Find an official with his boy assistant.

Rich people had statues in their gardens. Find two statues like this.

People poured tea from teapots and drank it from little bowls. Spot four teapots.

Lanterns were made of paper and had candles inside. Spot ten.

People used chopsticks to eat their food. Spot six pairs of chopsticks.

People went to temples but they also had shrines at home for worship. Find one.

Shrine

A type of pottery called porcelain was invented in China. Spot six jars like this one.

Screens were used as doors, or for decoration. They were often painted. Find one.

Indian wedding

At celebrations, people rode on elephants, on seats called howdahs. Find five elephants.

The holy man blessed the bride and groom. Can you see him?

Weavers made things from material. Find these woven things.

Red and gold wall hanging

Black and white cushion

Blue and green carpet

The palace had lovely gardens. Can you spot a gardener with a spade?

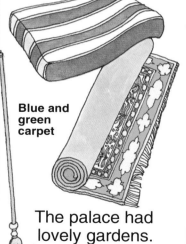

The emperor's golden throne was decorated with diamonds and rubies. Find it.

Can you see someone wearing this jewel in his turban?

The Mogul emperors in India were very rich. They lived in grand palaces like this one. Here, everyone is celebrating because the emperor's son is getting married. They are watching the wedding procession.

People wore gowns called jamas and trousers called piajamas. Spot a man in these clothes.

Yellow jama

Striped piajamas

Men wore turbans on their heads. Spot ten dark blue turbans.

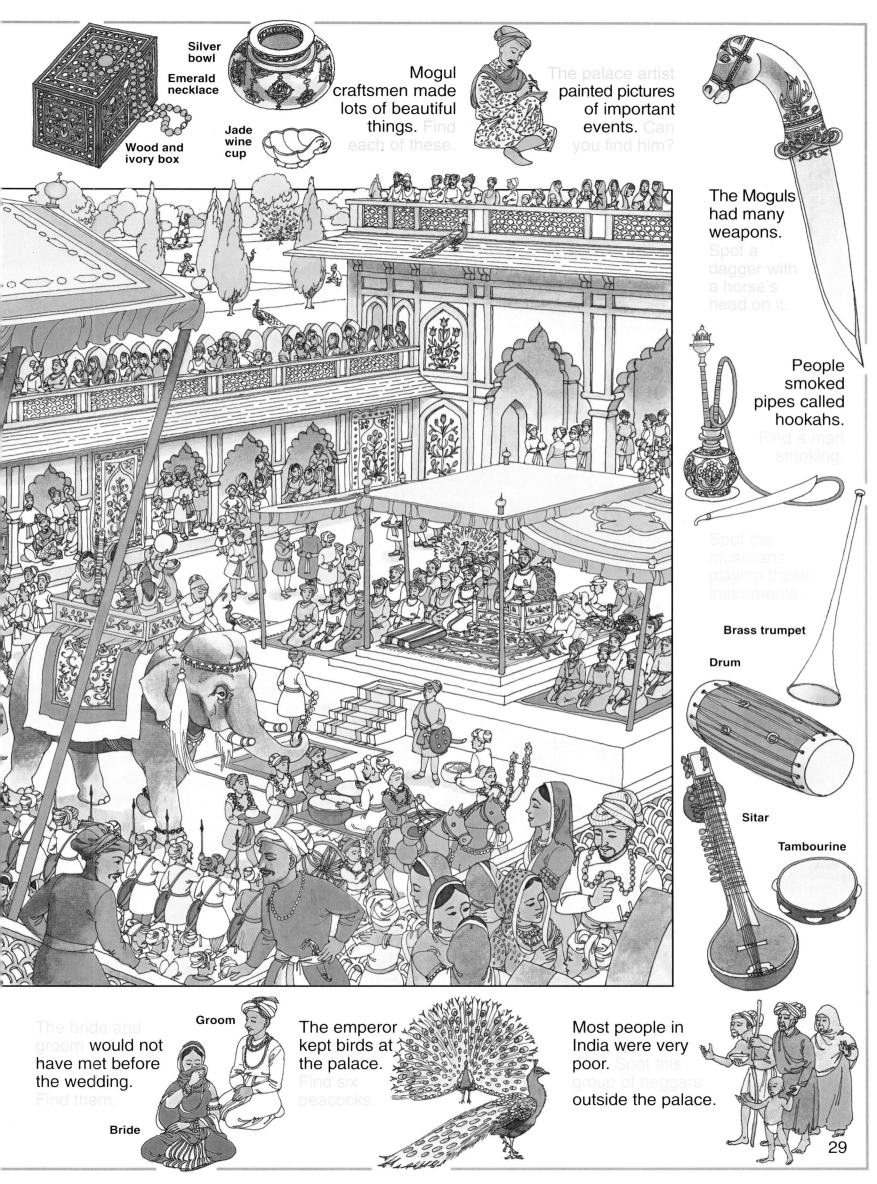

Silver bowl

Emerald necklace

Jade wine cup

Wood and ivory box

Mogul craftsmen made lots of beautiful things. Find each of these.

The palace artist painted pictures of important events. Can you find him?

The Moguls had many weapons. Spot a dagger with a horse's head on it.

People smoked pipes called hookahs. Find a man smoking.

Spot the musicians playing these instruments.

Brass trumpet

Drum

Sitar

Tambourine

The bride and groom would not have met before the wedding. Find them.

Groom

Bride

The emperor kept birds at the palace. Find six peacocks.

Most people in India were very poor. Spot this group of beggars outside the palace.

29

Busy ports

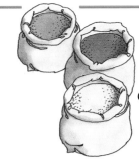

Spices, such as ginger and pepper, came from the East Indies. Spot three sacks of spices.

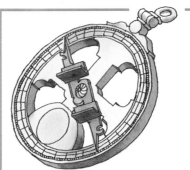

Sailors used astrolabes on voyages, to measure the height of stars. Can you see one?

There were all kinds of jobs to be done, even in port. Find these workers.

Rope-fitter

Sail mender

Carpenter

Most houses were tall and narrow, with a top part called a gable. Spot a green gable.

Goods were pulled up to storerooms in attics by machines called winches. Find three.

In the 1600s, Holland was a very rich country. Big ships, owned by merchants, sailed abroad to buy and sell goods.

This is a busy Dutch port. A big ship has just arrived home from a long voyage and is being unloaded.

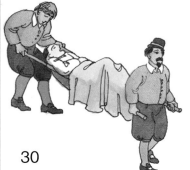

On long voyages, fresh food ran out, so many sailors became ill or died. Spot a sick sailor.

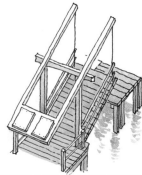

As well as roads, many Dutch towns had canals. Find an open bridge over a canal.

Tulips were rare and expensive. Can you see some?

Artists painted pictures of merchants and their families. Spot an artist.

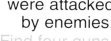
Ships had guns in case they were attacked by enemies. Find four guns.

The ship owner paid the crew after each voyage. Find him.

Many houses had stone fruit garlands, called swags, under their windows. Find six swags.

Sailors were often injured on voyages. Spot a sailor who has a wooden leg.

People played musical instruments at home. Find this virginal.

Rich people had servants. Spot the servants who are doing these jobs.

Hanging up laundry

Scrubbing floor tiles

Polishing silver

The telescope was invented in Holland. Spot a scientist using his telescope.

Many goods, such as tea and sugar, came from China, India or Africa. Find these things.

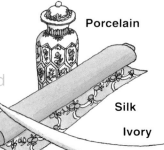
Porcelain

Silk

Ivory

Some rich people ran homes for orphans. Find two ladies collecting a homeless child.

31

Men wore wigs made of goat, horse or human hair. Can you see someone whose wig has fallen off?

Both men and women made up their faces. Spot someone checking his face in a pocket mirror.

Shoes often had fine embroidery and buckles. Find these shoes.

Musicians played dance music. Can you find a harpsichord?

Women curtsied and men bowed to the King. Spot the King.

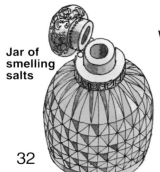

Jar of smelling salts

There were lots of clocks at the palace. Find two.

At the ball

The French King Louis XV lived in a fine palace at Versailles, near Paris. He entertained lots of rich people there. In this picture, everyone is at a ball, in a beautiful long room called the Hall of Mirrors.

Women often fainted from the heat. Spot a maid bringing smelling salts to revive her mistress.

The Hall of Mirrors had 17 arched mirrors. Find five of them.

Most people knew the steps for many different dances. Spot a dancer who has fallen over.

32

The King had hundreds of servants. Spot a servant pouring wine.

Dresses had very wide skirts. Find eight pink dresses with this pattern.

Men wore jackets, short trousers called breeches, and silk stockings. Spot a man in these clothes.

Women wore decorations in their hair. Find 11 wearing flowers in their hair.

Women stuck beauty spots on their faces. Find four women with beauty spots.

Hanging glass holders called chandeliers held candles. Can you find four others?

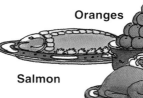

The palace was full of beautiful, expensive furniture. Can you see a couch?

Oranges

Salmon

Chicken

All kinds of tasty food was served at the ball. Spot these dishes.

People drank from crystal glasses. Can you spot someone spilling her wine?

Women carried pretty, painted fans. Find 11 women peeping over their fans.

There were rules about how to behave in front of the King. Spot someone who has misbehaved.

Richer people used carriages called hansom cabs as taxis. Find two.

Boats called barges were used to transport heavy goods on canals. Spot three.

People fetched water from pumps in the street. Spot someone pumping water.

Spot the people selling these things from carts or barrows.

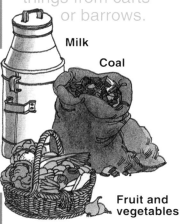

Milk

Coal

Fruit and vegetables

Factory town

Tray of matches

Children worked in mines, factories or on the streets. Spot a child selling matches.

This is a town in England. When big machines for making cloth and other things were invented, many country people moved to towns like this, to work in factories. The streets were noisy, crowded and dirty.

Homeless children and old people were sent to a harsh place called workhouse. Can you find one?

Steam trains carried passengers and goods all over the country at low cost. Spot a train.

Coal was the main fuel, so lots of people worked down coal mines. Spot six miners with lamps.

Miner's lamp

Sweep's brush

Chimney sweeps climbed up dark, sooty chimneys. Spot three sweeps.

Barber's

Shoemaker's

Tailor's

People bought things from small shops. Find these shops.

Streets were lit by gas lamps. Can you spot ten?

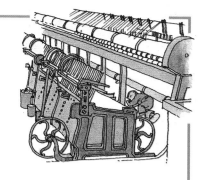

In factories, people worked long hours. Can you spot a tired worker who has fallen asleep?

Newspapers were on sale for people who could read. Spot a paper-seller.

The police tried to stop people from causing trouble or committing crimes. Spot six policemen.

Spot the people doing these jobs on the streets.

Selling pies

Lighting lamps

Selling flowers

Some orphans lived on the streets, stealing money or begging. Spot these beggars.

The filthy streets and houses were full of rats. Spot the rat-catcher doing his rounds.

The barrel organ player entertained people in the street. Can you see him?

Barrel organ

Prairie homes

The sheriff had to keep law and order. He wore a star-shaped badge. Find him.

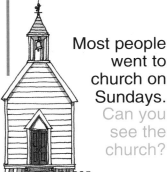

People who lived outside town came in to buy things. Spot someone buying this lamp.

There was only one school in town, with one teacher. Find the teacher.

Most people went to church on Sundays. Can you see the church?

There were no phones, but people sent messages by telegraph. Spot six telegraph poles.

For many years, the plains, or prairies, of North America were home to Native Americans. Then, settlers from the East took over the land, and built towns and railways. In this town, people are preparing for a holiday.

Some people kept on moving West. Spot a family loading their wagon.

The doctor treated people for illnesses or injuries. Can you see him?

Trains carried people, goods and cattle to other towns and cities. Find where the train stops.

Sometimes, robbers tried to steal money from the bank. Spot two.

Most men had guns. Can you find eight guns?

Handgun

Rifle

Men drank and played cards in a bar called a saloon. Spot the barman.

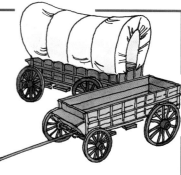
Wagons were used to carry heavy loads. Spot three with covers and three without.

People entertained each other with music. Find these instruments.

Accordion

Piano

Guitar

Some Native Americans lived near the town in areas called reservations. Spot four.

Many people worked on the railways. Spot five men laying new tracks.

Cowboys brought cattle into town. Spot eight other cowboys.

Richer people owned small carriages called buggies. Can you find two?

The local newspaper was printed once a week. Spot the newspaper office.

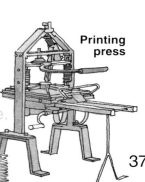
Printing press

37

Department stores

When the first department stores opened, people could buy all kinds of things in one building, instead of going to lots of shops.

Spot a fashion show going on in the women's clothes department.

All kinds of toys were sold in the toy department. Spot six of each of these.

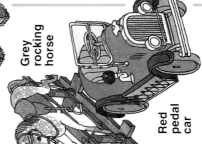

Teddy bear

Grey rocking horse

Red pedal car

Can you see where people are buying baby clothes?

Paperback books didn't cost much. Spot someone buying this book.

People played records on a phonograph. Spot someone choosing one.

The store had its own letter box where mail was collected. Find it.

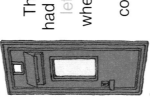

Jars of orange bonbons

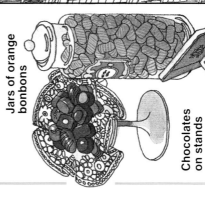

Chocolates on stands

Tins of toffees

Spot these things in the confectionery department.

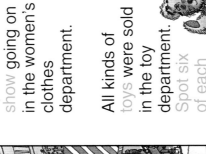

The store had a hairdressing salon. Spot three people having their hair cut. Can you see it?

Milkshakes were sold at a soda fountain.

Electric heaters warmed houses quickly. Spot six like this.

Radios called wirelesses were a new invention. Find three like this.

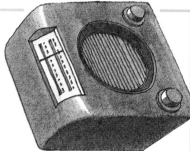

The glass and china department was full of fragile things. Spot someone who has broken a vase.

People could now buy many useful electrical goods. Spot three of each of these.

Washing machine

Stove

Vacuum cleaner

The store sold shoes for adults and children. Find two people trying on shoes.

Can you spot four attendants wearing uniforms like this?

There were phones in the store for people to use. Spot two.

Boxes of cereal

Strings of sausages

Bottles of tomato ketchup

Food was sold in the grocery department. Can you find these groceries?

39

Early people 4-5

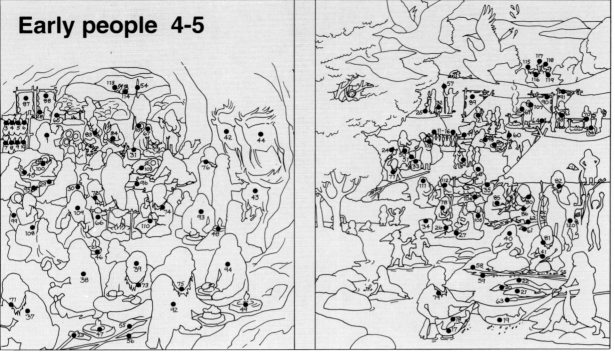

First farmers 6-7

Living in cities 8-9

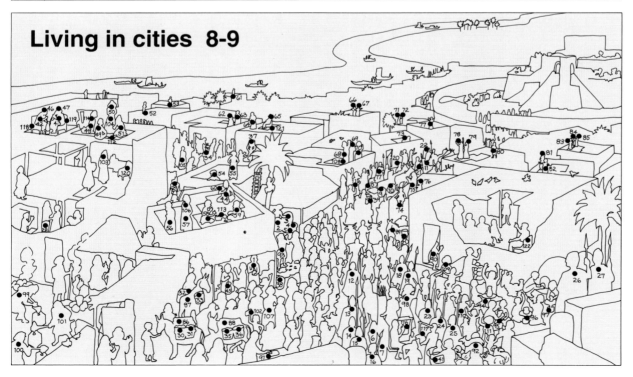

Storytellers 1 2
Fish 3 4 5 6 7 8
9 10 11 12 13 14
15 16 17 18 19
20 21 22
Axes 23 24
Digging sticks
25 26 27
Baskets
28 29 30 31 32
33 34 35 36
People chipping
away at flints
37 38 39 40 41
Deer pictures
42 43 44
Lamps
45 46 47 48 49
Leather bags
50 51 52
Child being
dressed 53
Spears 54 55 56
57 58 59 60 61
62 63 64
People cooking
65 66 67 68 69
70
Necklaces 71 72
73 74 75 76 77
78 79 80 81 82
People carving
antlers
83 84 85 86

Wooden racks
87 88 89 90 91
People making
paint 92 93 94
Skins being
scraped
95 96 97 98
Babies 99 100
101 102 103 104
105 106 107
People sewing
108 109 110 111
112
Wild deer
113 114 115 116
117 118 119
Boy who has
shot a bird 120

Ovens
1 2 3 4 5 6 7 8
Ladders 9 10 11
Women with
water pots 12 13
14 15 16 17 18
Cooking pots
19 20 21
People fishing
22 23 24 25
People making
pots 26 27
Men returning
from hunt 28 29
Spindles
30 31 32
Statue 33
Herders
34 35 36 37
Women grinding
38 39 40 41
Dogs 42 43 44
45 46 47 48 49
Children scaring
birds 50 51 52 53
Geese 54 55 56
57 58 59 60 61
62 63 64
Cattle 65 66 67
68 69 70 71 72
73 74 75 76 77
78 79 80
Pigs 81 82 83 84
85 86

Piglets 87 88 89
90 91 92
Goats
93 94 95 96
Sheep
97 98 99 100
101 102 103 104
105 106 107 108
109 110 111 112
113 114 115 116
Looms
117 118 119
Men mending
wall 120 121
Baskets
122 123 124 125
126 127 128
Roof on fire 129
Sickles 130 131
132 133 134

Scribe 1
Wheels 2 3 4 5 6
7 8 9 10 11
Soldiers 12 13
14 15 16 17 18
19 20 21 22 23
24 25 26 27
Baskets
28 29 30 31 32
33 34 35 36 37
38 39 40 41
People using
straws
42 43 44 45
People on roofs
46 47 48 49 50
51 52 53 54 55
56 57 58 59 60
61 62 63 64 65
66 67 68 69 70
71 72 73 74 75
76 77 78 79 80
81 82 83 84 85
Donkeys with
packs
86 87 88 89
Late boy 90
Stone seal 91
Farmer with
sheep 92
Person who has
broken jar 93
Potter's wheels
94 95 96 97

King 98
Metalsmiths
99 100 101
Messenger 102
Women in blue
dresses 103 104
105 106 107 108
109 110 111
Pairs of men
playing game
112 113
People playing
harps 114 115
116 117
Chairs 118 119
120 121 122

Pyramids 10-11

Going into battle 12-13

At the market 14-15

Dogs 1 2 3 4 5
People polishing
6 7 8 9
Architect 10
Doctor 11
Monkey 12
Pyramid models
13 14
Chisels 15 16 17
18 19 20
King 21
Hawks 22 23 24
25 26 27 28
Saws 29 30 31
Scribes 32 33 34
35 36 37
Man with hole in
basket 38
Overseer 39
Oil jars
40 41 42 43
Queen 44
Measuring
instruments
45 46 47 48 49
Hammers 50 51
52 53 54 55
Sleds 56 57 58
59 60 61 62 63 64
Men using poles
65 66 67 68 69 70
71 72
Person falling off
ramp 73

Siege engines
1 2 3 4 5
Swimming
horses 6 7 8 9
Bows 10 11 12
13 14 15 16 17
18 19 20 21
Soldiers putting
on boots
22 23 24 25
Soldiers with
sacks
26 27 28 29 30
Captives 31 32
33 34 35 36 37
Yellow cloths
38 39 40 41
People falling
42 43 44 45 46
47 48
Boats
49 50 51 52
Scribes 53 54
Soldiers on white
horses 55 56
Slings 57 58 59
60 61 62 63 64
Broken spear 65
Ladders
66 67 68 69 70
71 72 73
King 74
Person who has
let go of float 75

Person who has
dropped shield
76
Mother giving
drink to child 77
Sheep 78 79 80
81 82 83 84
Swords 85 86 87
88 89 90 91 92
93 94 95 96 97
98 99

Man dropping his
money 1
Weighing scales
2 3 4 5 6 7
Person eating
olives 8
Dogs 9 10 11 12
Slave carrying too
much shopping 13
Soldiers
14 15 16 17 18
Cats 19 20 21 22
People who have
been to fish stall
23 24 25 26
Hats
27 28 29 30 31
Two-handled jars
32 33 34 35 36
Actors 37 38 39
Escaping slave 40
Banker 41
Lamp stall 42
Statues 43 44
Philosophers 45 46
People carrying
sandals 47 48 49
People drinking
wine 50 51 52 53
Children playing
with hoops
54 55 56
Man who hates
his haircut 57

The bath house 16-17

People having a massage 1 2 3 4
People lifting weights 5 6 7 8 9
Person stealing clothes 10
Caldarium 11
Statue 12
Gladiator 13
Women 14 15 16 17 18.
Man who has forgotten sandals 19
Thief 20
Library 21
Slave who has fainted 22
Person putting on toga 23
Frigidarium 24
Food trays 25 26
Attendant with towels 27
Mosaic floor 28
Soldiers 29 30 31 32 33 34 35 36
Oil flasks 37 38 39 40 41 42 43 44 45 46 47
Complaining man 48
Strigils 49 50 51 52 53

Winter feasts 18-19

Person doing up brooch 1
People fetching wood 2 3
Spoons 4 5 6 7 8 9 10 11 12 13 14 15
Person with torn tunic 16
Poet 17
Chief 18
Child hiding behind tapestry 19
Person falling off stool 20
Barrels 21 22 23 24 25 26 27
Fighting dogs 28 29
Open chest 30
Dried fish 31 32 33 34 35 36 37 38 39 40
Drinking horns 41 42 43 44 45 46 47 48 49 50 51 52
Lamps 53 54 55 56 57
Servant with pile of bowls 58
Person stirring cauldron 59

Pair of acrobats 60
Jugs 61 62 63 64 65 66
Swords 67 68 69 70 71
Loom 72

Village life 20-21

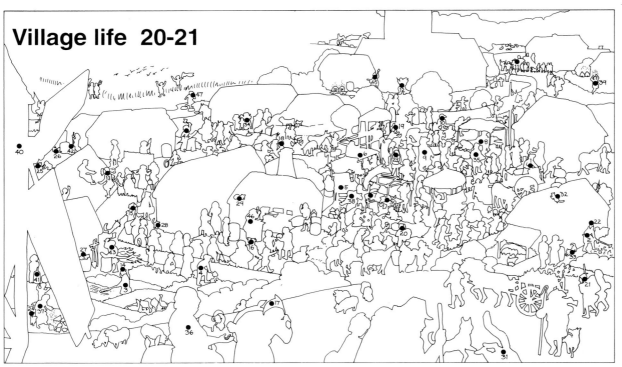

Merchant unloading wine 1
Person using hoe 2
Person using rake 3
Person using spade 4
Tables 5 6 7 8
Dancing bear 9
Person in stocks 10
Lord 11
Priest 12
Pointed hoods 13 14 15 16 17 18 19 20 21 22
Cheeses 23
Cats 24 25 26 27 28 29 30 31 32 33
Woman picking lice from hair 34
Person selling things from a tray 35
Miller 36
People feeding chickens 37 38
Man being chased by bees 39
Windmill 40
Churns 41 42

People chopping wood 43 44 45
Blacksmith 46
Person using stepping stones 47

Castle life 22-23

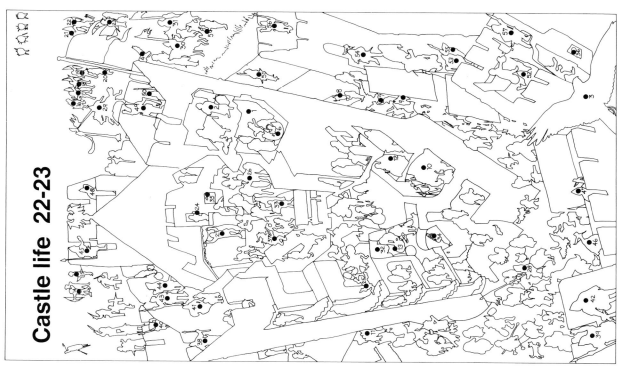

Bed 1
Lord counting money 2
Falcons 3 4 5
Person in a bathtub 6
Horses looking out of stables 7 8 9
Guardroom 10
Candlemaker 11
Chapel 12
Well 13
Archers 14 15 16 17 18 19 20 21 22 23
Person looking out of window 24
Person falling down stairs 25
Group of minstrels 26
Person hanging a tapestry 27
Knights on horseback 28 29 30 31
Storeroom 32
Servant with tray of goblets 33
Prisoner in chains 34
Toilets 35 36
Jester 37

Guards on battlements 38 39 40 41 42 43 44 45 46 47 48 49 50 51 52 53 54 55 56 57

Inca homes 24-25

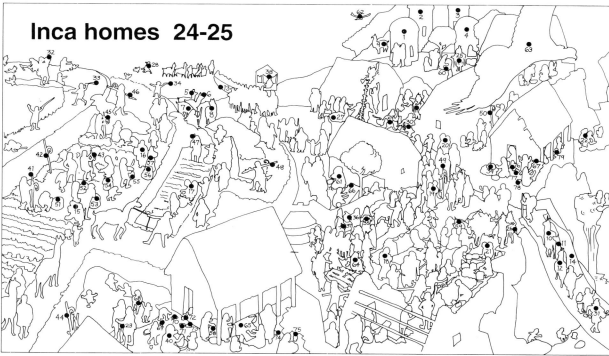

Storehouses 1 2 3 4
Alpacas 5 6 7 8 9 10 11 12
Bridges 13 14
Babies 15 16 17 18 19 20 21 22
Quipus 23 24 25 26
Llama sitting down 27
Chasquis 28 29 30 31
Pototo 32
Slings 33 34
Panpipes 35
Drum 36
Flute 37
Emperor 38
Cooking pot 39
Woman grinding 40
Digging sticks 41 42 43 44 45 46 47 48 49 50
Sacks of potatoes 51 52 53 54 55 56 57 58 59 60
Person making chicha drink 61
Condors 62 63
Person putting on sandals 64

Looms 65 66 67
Guinea pigs 68 69 70 71 72 73 74 75 76 77 78 79

A Chinese party 26-27

Dragon pictures 1 2 3 4 5 6 7 8
Chair covers 9 10 11 12
Half-finished bowl of rice 13
Incense burner 14
Dogs 15 16 17 18 19 20 21
Lacquered trays 22 23 24 25 26 27 28
Gardener and his children 29
Drum 30
Gong 31
Flute 32
Shrine 33
Jars 34 35 36 37 38 39
Screen 40
Pairs of chopsticks 41 42 43 44 45 46
Lanterns 47 48 49 50 51 52 53 54 55 56
Teapots 57 58 59 60
Statues 61 62
Official with boy assistant 63
Paintings 64 65

Servant lighting a firework 66
Red robes 67 68 69 70 71 72 73 74
Fans 75 76 77

43

Indian wedding 28-29

Elephants
1 2 3 4 5
Holy man 6
Red and gold
wall hanging 7
Black and white
cushion 8
Blue and green
carpet 9
Gardener with
spade 10
Throne 11
Man in yellow
jama and striped
piajamas 12
Dark blue
turbans
13 14 15 16 17
18 19 20 21 22
Bride 23
Groom 24
Peacocks 25 26
27 28 29 30
Group of
beggars 31
Musician playing
sitar 32
Musician playing
tambourine 33
Musician playing
drum 34
Musician playing
brass trumpet 35
Man smoking 36

Dagger with
horse's head 37
Palace artist 38
Jade wine cup 39
Silver bowl 40
Emerald
necklace 41
Wood and ivory
box 42
Person wearing
turban jewel 43

Busy ports 30-31

Astrolabe 1
Rope-fitter 2
Sail mender 3
Carpenter 4
Green gable 5
Winches 6 7 8
Sick sailor 9
Open bridge 10
Tulips 11
Scientist using
telescope 12
Ivory 13
Silk 14
Porcelain 15
Ladies collecting
orphan 16
Servant polishing
silver 17
Servant
scrubbing floor
tiles 18
Servant hanging
up laundry 19
Virginal 20
Sailor with
wooden leg 21
Swags 22 23 24
25 26 27
Ship owner 28
Guns
29 30 31 32
Artist 33
Sacks of spices
34 35 36

At the ball 32-33

Person whose
wig has fallen off
1
Person checking
his face in a
pocket mirror 2
Embroidered
pink shoes 3
Harpsichord 4
King 5
Maid bringing
smelling salts to
her mistress 6
Arched mirrors
7 8 9 10 11
Dancer who has
fallen over 12
Person spilling
wine 13
Women peeping
over fans 14 15
16 17 18 19 20
21 22 23 24
Person who has
misbehaved 25
Chicken 26
Salmon 27
Oranges 28
Couch 29
Chandeliers
30 31 32 33 34
Women with
beauty spots
35 36 37 38

Women wearing
flowers in their
hair 39 40 41 42
43 44 45 46 47
48 49
Man in blue
jacket and green
breeches 50
Pink dresses
51 52 53 54 55
56 57 58
Servant pouring
wine 59
Clocks 60 61

Factory town 34-35

Hansom cabs 1 2
Barges 3 4 5
Person pumping water 6
Person selling coal 7
Person selling fruit and vegetables 8
Person selling milk 9
Workhouse 10
Train 11
Miners 12 13 14 15 16 17
Beggars 18
Rat-catcher 19
Barrel organ player 20
Person selling flowers 21
Person lighting lamps 22
Person selling pies 23
Policemen 24 25 26 27 28 29
Paper-seller 30
Sleeping factory worker 31
Gas lamps 32 33 34 35 36 37 38 39 40 41

Tailor's 42
Barber's 43
Shoemaker's 44
Chimney sweeps 45 46 47
Child selling matches 48

Prairie homes 36-37

Sheriff 1
Person buying lamp 2
Teacher 3
Church 4
Telegraph poles 5 6 7 8 9 10
Family loading their wagon 11
Doctor 12
Place where train stops 13
Cowboys 14 15 16 17 18 19 20 21 22
Buggies 23 24
Newspaper office 25
Men laying new tracks 26 27 28 29 30
Native Americans 31 32 33 34
Guitar 35
Piano 36
Accordion 37
Wagons with covers 38 39 40
Wagons without covers 41 42 43
Barman 44
Guns 45 46 47 48 49 50 51 52

Robbers 53 54
Blacksmith 55

Department stores 38-39

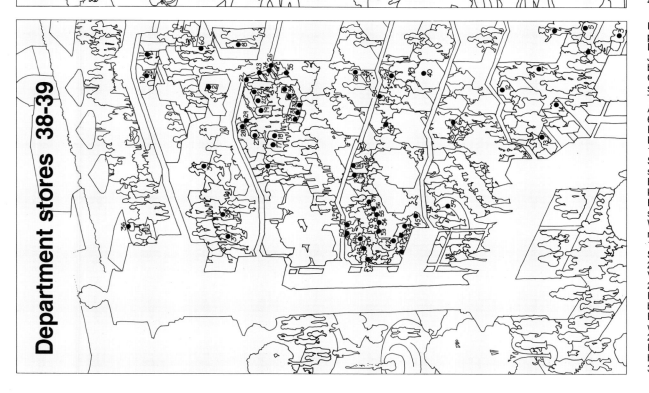

Person choosing phonograph 1
Letter box 2
Jars of orange bonbons 3
Chocolates on stands 4
Tins of toffees 5
Attendants 6 7 8 9
Phones 10 11
Boxes of cereal 12
Strings of sausages 13
Bottles of tomato ketchup 14
People trying on shoes 15 16
Washing machines 17 18 19
Stoves 20 21 22
Vacuum cleaners 23 24 25
Person who has broken a vase 26
Brown square wirelesses 27 28 29
Pink electric heaters 30 31 32 33 34 35

Soda fountain 36
People having their hair cut 37 38 39
Place where people are buying baby clothes 40
Red pedal cars 41 42 43 44 45 46
Grey rocking horses 47 48 49 50 51 52
Teddy bears 53 54 55 56 57 58
Fashion show 59
Person buying orange book 60

What are they doing?

You can find each of these people somewhere in the little pictures earlier in the book. To do this puzzle, you'll need to look back and find where they come from.

1. Which of these people is painting a picture?

A B C D E F

2. Which of these children is late for school?

A B C D E F

3. Which of these people is going into battle?

A B C D E F G

4. Which of these women is a queen?

A B C D E F G

5. Which of these people is telling a story?

A B C D E F

6. Which of these pairs of people is in the middle of an argument?

A B C D E

The answers are on page 48.

Index

Answers to the puzzle on page 46: 1C 2F 3A 4F 5B 6D

With thanks to:
Mr Fred Redding, Company Archivist, Selfridges, London
The Archive Departments at Harrods Ltd and John Lewis Partnership
Rachael Swann for checking puzzles